ALBERT KERR

DEBT SECRETS

The Ultimate Guide on How to Organize Your Debt, Learn the Effective Strategies and Useful Tips on How to Track Your Money and Pay Your Debts

Descrierea CIP a Bibliotecii Naţionale a României
ALBERT KERR
    DEBT SECRETS. The Ultimate Guide on How to Organize Your Debt, Learn the Effective Strategies and Useful Tips on How to Track Your Money and Pay Your Debts / Albert Kerr – Bucharest: Editura My Ebook, 2021
    ISBN

ALBERT KERR

DEBT SECRETS

The Ultimate Guide on How to Organize Your Debt, Learn the Effective Strategies and Useful Tips on How to Track Your Money and Pay Your Debts

My Ebook Publishing House
Bucharest, 2021

TABLE OF CONTENTS

FOREWORD

Whether you are married or single, taking charge of your overall finances may feel like a part-time job. Some easy ideas can help you streamline your time, organize your finances, and reduce the stress of debt and overall money matters.

Organizing Debts For Better Money Management
Know Where Your Money Goes And Keep More Of It

CHAPTER 1

ORGANIZE THE PAPER

Synopsis

When the mail arrives, make certain it goes in one place. Lost bills can be the cause of uninvited late fees and may damage your credit rating. Whether it's a drawer, a box, or a file, be ordered and make certain other people in the household do the same. Size is likewise important. If you get a lot of mail, utilize an area that won't get filled up too fast.

Make It Neat

Your bills come every month whether you wish them to or not. Setting them in a cubby hole somewhere and dealing with them later may lead you to draw a blank about their maturity date. When this occurs you wind up being forced to pay a late fee. If you're willing to get organized, you are able to get your bills paid on time and never have to fret about incurring a late fee. This might take a little bit of time to set up, but only a couple of extra minutes per week to sustain.

Make sure you open your bills. A lot of bills come with unneeded inserts that just take up room in the place where you store your bills. Take out any inserts and recycle them with the outer envelope at once. This keeps clutter from stacking up and taking your focus off of the bill itself. Now take the bill and put it under the fold of the return envelope.

You are able to label 4 plastic bins so that each one makes up a week of the month. You are able to simply label them "Week 1," "Week 2," "Week 3," and "Week 4." Now take your prepared bills and find out the maturity date. If the maturity date is the 8th of the month, the bill goes in the week 2 bin. If the maturity date is the twentieth, the bill goes in the bin for week 3.

Do this with all of your bills and then place the bins on top of one another in order. When week 1 rolls around, take your bills out and pay them. Then put the bin on the bottom of the pile so that the week 2 bills are ready for you the next week.

Finally once your bills are paid, you nevertheless have your financial statements to deal with. You want to keep them coordinated as well so that you are able to quickly locate them if you need to.

Buy a thirteen pocket file folder. Mark the first twelve pockets with the calendar months of the year. The last pocket can be marked "taxes." Place your monthly financial statements into the pocket for that certain month.

When the year is complete, you are able to label the file folder with the year on the front and store it just in case you ever get audited.

CHAPTER 2

MANAGE YOUR MONEY TO STAY
ON SCHEDULE

Synopsis

Bill paying may be simplified if it's done at scheduled times during the month as we discussed. Depending upon how many bills you get, you are able to establish set times monthly so none of your bills will be late. If you're paying bills as you receive them, chances are you're spending a bit much time in front of the checkbook. Although bills might say "Payable Upon Receipt", there's always a grace period. Call the creditor to discover when they need to get payment before the bill is considered late and use these tips.

Keep Up

Wouldn't matters just be more comfortable if everybody had an accountant to handle all the financial matters in his life? For those who can not afford to maintain an accountant on retainer, you need to answer as your own accountant and discover how to supervise your money, where it goes, and what it's for.

Here are a few ideas to help you if you're a tad bit uncertain how to go about addressing the money matters.

As previously stated, organize. It is all-important for your bills and receipts to be organized and in order. This is because you may wind up paying the incorrect amounts and losing track of your list of costs. As stated in chapter 1, one way to go about doing this would be to keep a bin or a file folder of each week that a bill is due, and keep the receipts filed also. Let's suppose you pay for water, electricity and cable television monthly. Put them all in their respective bins according to due date, which should be updated every time you open your bills.

Make sure you appropriate funds every payday. On payday, head toward your stack of bins and figure out the revenue you need to reserve for each bill that you have to pay.

Make this your top priority. Then set aside a particular amount every payday, which should go to a savings account. The remainder would now be your pocket money, or your so-called disposable income.

Pay for bills online or consolidate bill payments. Acquaint yourself with how to pay for your bills online. A few banks and financial institutions actually let you consolidate your bills into merely one payment. Not only will this save you the time and energy, but it would likewise be a beneficial way for you to track your bills, as you'll be able to see a record of all the payments you've made. Don't blow your time any longer by going to the physical building and paying each bill over the counter. It would be easier and much more efficient for you if you are able to do it from the comfort of your own home or office.

You can always discuss your monthly bills with your loved ones, if needed. If for a certain month, you notice that your water bill is exceptionally higher than the former months, advise your family members to attempt to save on consumption. If you're open with your loved ones about this, they'll better value money and finances, and they may begin helping out through simple ways, like unplugging appliances when not in use.

Make sure you review your bills from time to time. Make certain that you don't miss out on any payments to prevent penalty charges, and to prevent messing up your budget. Begin with a fresh start every month without any leftover accounts payable, so your bills don't pile up.

The magic to managing your finances and paying bills on time is prioritization and organization. Sure, everybody wants to purchase the newest car, gadget, clothes, or jewelry. But, bills are a fact of life. Rent payments are a fact of life. Mortgage payments are a fact of life. You need to be able to see where your money goes, and be organized enough to know how much should be spent for any certain things and how much is left over.

CHAPTER 3

CHECK YOUR STATEMENTS

Synopsis

Most individuals capitalize on low interest charge card offers but never read their statements when paying the bill. Charge cards are notorious for utilizing low interest as bait for fresh clients then switching to higher rates after a couple of months. Make a habit of looking at your statement cautiously to see what rate of interest you're paying monthly and if any transaction fees have been applied. If the rate increases or a transaction fee shows up on your statement, a simple call to the charge card company can often be beneficial in resolving the matter. If not, try to swap your money to a more positive rate.

Understand It

Paying delinquent interest on your charge card monthly can total up to an immense sum at the end of the year, that is, if you are able to track your payments. It may be frustrating to forever keep looking for charge card bills that you know came in the mail but can't remember where you put them precisely. Before you know it, you'll either make another late payment or worse, altogether forget to pay them. To obtain savings and increase your credit rating, it will take some effort on your part to organize and keep a record of your charge card bills and payments.

Make sure you look at all your charge cards and make a list of them. Next gather all your charge card bills. Look at the statements and check the dates when the payments are owed. List each date beside your charge card list and use the bin method in chapter 1. This way you'll know which charge card bills you are able to expect in a billing cycle and make a schedule later.

Put your charge card bills into separate bins so you that you can't miss seeing them. Place a stapler, paper clips and pens close to where you keep the bins or file folders.

Make sure you keep a small basket or box where you are able to drop all your receipts each time you shop. Make certain that you regularly place all your receipts in this container. At the end of the week, make it a habit to go through all your purchase receipts and sort them in separate files per charge card. Clip them together for easier management and access.

When a charge card bill comes in, check the statement. Compare the itemized list of purchases that you've made against all the receipts that you have saved and separated. This will help you to keep track of your purchases, the amount you paid against what is reflected in your charge card bill and make complaints if you discover discrepancies, whether in your purchases or payments. See to it that you check each charge card bill as soon as it comes in and that the bill is always in the correct bin for timely payment.

Attach the receipts to each statement. Write the word "PAID" and a date on those bills that you've paid. You might have to do this a couple of times if you are able to only manage to pay the lower limit.

Alternate the utilization of your charge cards based on their billing cycles. This way you don't get deluged with several statements in the middle and end of the month.

Make a little record, either on paper or do one utilizing a spreadsheet. Label each column with the charge card name, the total balance, the due date, the lower limit payment, the amount you paid off, the current balance and when you paid them. Place this with your bins or folders and regularly cross off those that you've paid in full. You are able to then anticipate what is due and see those that you've paid fully.

Organizing your charge card bills will keep your regular payments on track, exempting you from worry and giving you some savings. Keep all your charge card bills for at least one year, for audit and quick reference to check purchases and payments. You might find that some charge cards have outrageous surcharges and are worth canceling.

CHAPTER 4

USE AUTOMATIC PAYMENTS

Synopsis

Many banks offer a way to automatically subtract money from your account to pay creditors. Additionally, the creditors commonly offer a lower rate of interest when you sign on for this payment choice as they get their money faster and not late. Think about it as one fewer check to write, envelope to lick and stamp to purchase. Just make certain you record the subtraction when the automatic payment is scheduled or you run the risk of bouncing other checks.

Pay Online

Online bill pay may help you manage your bills without being forced to worry about paper bills and checks. We will cover the various types of online bill pay and how you are able to set up online bill pay fast and easy. Once you're up and running, you are able to spend more time on the fun things in life.

First we'll want to make certain we know what type of online bill pay you truly have available.

Respective different services are described as online bill pay:

➤ Online bill pay provided by your bank

➤ Online bill pay provided by your service providers (phone company, mortgage company, and so forth)

The beginning type of online bill pay (online bill pay provided by your bank) is a service that sends off money out of your bank account to whomever you wish. In a few cases these online bill pay services will in reality print a check and mail it to the recipient. If the company you prefer to send payments to is setup inside the banks system, the bank will merely transfer the money electronically when you utilize online bill pay.

To establish this type of online bill pay you'll likely just need a copy of the bill that your service provider sends out to you. Establish a new payee in the name of that company at your online bill pay site. Copy the address and your account number, and enter that data likewise. Each time you would like to pay you'll just put in the amount of the bill and you're done. The bank will print and mail a check that will pull revenue from your account.

To be secure, you should countercheck with the payees if they have particular instructions for receiving payments thru online bill pay. Some payees won't recognize the check (as it was printed by the online bill pay service). In this case, they might give you an alternate address or other directions.

The 2nd type of online bill pay (online bill pay provided by your service providers) is a service that will only let you pay one company – like your phone service for instance.

To establish online bill pay with the telephone company, you'll need to furnish the company a voided check and one or two forms and authorizations. The procedure is really similar to direct deposit but they call it online bill pay or ACH debit.

When you've set things up, you are able to pay your bill without being forced to use paper checks or the mail.

Automatic Bill Pay Online

If you truly like to automate matters so that you don't have to think about them, you are able to automate online bill pay. Virtually all online bill pay services will let you establish recurring payments. For instance, you are able to have the online bill pay service attend to your phone bill each month or your insurance quarterly.

A different way you are able to let online bill pay keep going on auto-pilot is to let your service providers pull money out of your account without you being forced to click anyplace. Put differently, the service supplier just "asks" the online bill pay company for payment and the payment is made with no activity on your part. If you authorize these forms of payments, make certain you've a good handle on your budget and usable funds.

Online bill pay may truly make your life easier. Once you set it up, you are able to reduce lost payments and the quantity of time you spend shuffling papers.

CHAPTER 5

COMPUTERIZE

Synopsis

Utilizing a software program is a convenient way to organize your finances. Whether it's Quicken®, Microsoft Money® or a different package, these simple -to- utilize programs make bill paying and bank reconciliation a breeze. Computer checks may be ordered almost anyplace and fit right into most printers. Once the checks are printed, all of the data is automatically recorded in your electronic checkbook. Moreover, many banks have direct downloads into these software packages so when money is deposited or drawn off, the transaction is entered directly onto your computer. And, when it comes time to do taxes, it couldn't be simpler.

Quicken

The reason a lot of individuals decide to purchase a computer is to more adeptly organize their personal finances or even execute a small business. Quicken not only organizes your checking account but it helps you pay bills, keep track of tax write-offs and develop budgets, financial statements and reports.

Quicken for Windows capitalizes on the Windows user-friendly environment. In Quicken, users may trigger the Activities menu to produce new accounts, write checks, pay charge card bills, update balances, establish budgets, create registers or activate an on-screen calculator. With Quicken you are able to print checks utilizing your computer's printer or use electronic payment to automatically send payments using your computer, modem and phone line.

When you first establish a Quicken bank account you'll discover yourself in the Register window where all transactions are registered. These transactions include hand written checks or printed by computer, ATM transactions, deposits, account fees and interest and service charges.

When producing a Quicken bank account, the Register window acts as a check register like your paper check register.

25

When you record a check in Write Checks, it shows up in the check register and becomes a lasting part of your records. Your balance is updated automatically. Just state what it's for, telephone bill, foodstuffs, piano lessons, charity, whatever and then you are able to produce reports showing precisely where your money goes. Once you get your monthly bank statement, you are able to quickly reconcile it with your Quicken check register.

The Quicken charge card register enables you to computerize your charge card records. It can likewise help you keep track of your investitures in stocks, bonds, mutual funds and additional investments that waver in price. However this is an advanced feature so take your time to learn it.

Categories are a different handy characteristic. A category is a label that you are able to put on a transaction that helps you track how much you're spending on certain items. For home users, you may have expense classes like food, mortgage, medical fees, utilities and so forth. Your revenue categories may include items like salary, bonuses, maternity leave pay and so forth.

By categorizing transactions you are able to make a report that totals all tax-related income and expenses by class for every month in a year. Some reports are particularly designed to sort and tally transactions by classes. For instance, you are able to track how much you spend monthly on food or, if you're a small business, you are able to discover what your top 3 sources of revenue are. Category names, which you establish before entering transactions or as you enter, may be very particular or general. You are able to even categorize every transaction if you want.

You can use pre-formatted reports. These reports may help you analyze your finances in detail. You are able to produce reports that show your spending, budget, tax-deductible expenses, cash flow, accounts payable and so forth.

Stored transactions are among the most useful timesavers. Quicken can memorize any repeating checks or additional transactions like mortgage payments, utility bills, payroll deposits and electronic payments to send. When you prefer to enter a memorized transaction, just tell Quicken which one you require and it enters it into the register for you.

The CheckFree feature lets you send payment instructions to CheckFree thru modem. Then CheckFree sends the payment to any person, organization or corporation in the U.S. per your request. To pay for bills you start by entering an electronic payment transaction, very much like entering a paper check in the Write Checks or Register window. You are able to also write payroll checks for business use.

As you are able to see, Quicken comes in handy. It supplies you with easy-to-use tools for computerizing your check book, budget, charge card records, investments and much more. There are several programs available out there... this one was just used a basic example of how the programs work.

CHAPTER 6

DIRECT DEPOSIT

Synopsis

Many employers have direct deposit or are catching on. Even Unemployment Compensation provides direct deposit as a choice to receive benefit checks. On payday, the amount of your paycheck arrives in your account and is promptly available.

Directly In The Bank

Direct deposit enables you to handily move money electronically without mailing or signing any checks over to the bank. With direct deposit, your money seems to get to your account faster. When you utilize it for your paycheck, you won't have to go to the bank to cash or deposit your paycheck ever again.

Here's how to establish direct deposit:

Get hold of the originator of the payment. For instance, if you want your paycheck to be direct deposited, get hold of the Human Resources or the Payroll department of your company. The United States Government offers direct deposit for Social Security payments and tax refunds; get hold of them directly about this service. A few investment and insurance payments might also be directly deposited. Get hold of whoever will be paying you to ask about direct deposit.

Next complete a direct deposit form. This ought to be provided by the organization or person that is paying you. You'll need your bank's routing number, which is published on your checks or can be gotten from your bank. It might also be called an ABA number or a 'routing transit' number, and is a singular identifier for your certain bank. You'll in addition need your account number, which describes your certain account at that certain bank. You are able to have the funds set up to direct deposit into your regular checking or savings account, or establish a special account for these funds. Finally, the form might require the physical address of the bank to which payment ought to be sent, even though it will be sent out electronically.

Additional required info might include your name, address, telephone number, or social security number.

Now you send off the form to the payor. Send this form back to the organization or person that will be paying you. A few in addition call for a voided check to verify that your routing number and bank account number is right. Make certain to clearly mark this check as VOID prior to sending it. A few companies might also be set up to take this data online or over the phone.

Direct deposit is a handy way to get your money. With just a couple of short forms, you are able to wipe out a lot of paperwork and fuss later on. You'll never lose a paycheck or unintentionally wash it in your pants pocket again, as there are no paper checks to be lost or stolen. The payments will be in your account without you having to make a trip to the bank to deposit the check.

It generally takes a couple of weeks to institute and is well worth the wait. All the same, you still should get a payment stub from your employer or person paying you, listing the itemized deductions for that period or the amount and intention of the check.

CHAPTER 7

ACQUIRE OVERDRAFT PROTECTION

Synopsis

Many banks have a service where, if you run the chance of bouncing a check, the money will come from a different source. For a token fee, the bank will link your checking account to a savings, money market, or charge card so the plethora of bouncing a check will be avoided.

Protection

It only takes a moment or two to maintain the serenity that overdraft coverage can provide.

You should know however that beginning soon, banks and credit unions will no longer be allowed to bill overdraft fees unless clients sign up for the service. Do nothing, and you may have a purchase declined at the register. On the other hand, you will not find yourself burdened with unforeseen fees.

With fee - founded overdraft services, your bank will back you when a debit card buy or ATM withdrawal goes past the sum of money in your current account. Banks state this service saves clients from embarrassment and allows for a quick source of emergency money. However the price of saving your dignity can be high. As most banks bill a flat fee for overdrafts, a $2 overdraft for a cup of coffee may cost you $35. And once you've passed your limit, every buy you do might have a fee.

In the past, a lot of banks automatically listed clients in overdraft coverage. But under fresh federal rules, beginning July 1, banks will be expected to get new customers' permission prior to charging fees to back ATM and debit card overdrafts. Beginning Aug. 15, they will be banned from billing overdraft fees to existing clients unless they choose the service.

You should know that, there are other, less-costly means to avoid having your debit card declined at the supermarket, including:

➢ Associate your checking account to a savings account. A lot of banks and credit unions provide this service for clients who have savings accounts. If you overdraw your checking account, revenue in your savings account is applied to cover the transaction. Banks commonly charge a fee to shift the money, but it's commonly $5 to $10 — a good deal lower than the fee billed by standard overdraft service programs.

➢ Associate your account to a charge card. In this case, an advance from your charge card will be utilized to cover the overdraft. You'll pay interest — and the rate for charge card advances is commonly higher than the rate for purchases — However if you pay the balance off fast, you'll likely still pay less than you'd give in overdraft fees.

➢ Establish an overdraft credit line with your bank or credit union. You'll need to apply for a credit line, and clients with mediocre credit might not qualify. However if you're eligible, this may provide a much less expensive sort of overdraft protection than fee-based coverage.

➢ Establish low-balance alarms. Knowledge is the most efficient means to protect yourself against overdrafts. A lot of financial institutions will send you an e-mail or text once your balance arrives at the danger zone.

Instead, regularly monitoring your checking account will help you prevent spending money you don't have. You might want to set up an online account and review it daily. That sort of examination will bring you face to face with the realism of your spending.

CHAPTER 8

GET RID OF UNUSED ACCOUNTS

Synopsis

Whether it's a charge card or bank account, write a letter calling for the account to be formally closed. Not only will this better your credit score, it's a useful way to prevent money from being scattered all over the place. Don't let department stores and charge card companies lure you into opening fresh accounts by offering positive interest rates and purchase discounts. It's simple for credit to get out of control by taking every credit offer that comes along.

Cancel It

You would like to cancel your charge card. Before you gather up your scissors, know this: Canceling a charge card correctly involves more than simply clipping it in two. It calls for you following some necessary steps.

You need to know that depending upon your total available credit, closing an account may hurt your credit score. To close card accounts without affecting one's credit score, you need only have "0" balances on your credit report for all of your active charge cards. That's because if you have "0" balances your credit use rate is therefore "0", and you can't raise it and possibly harm your score by closing one or more of the active charge accounts.

As well, the age of a charge card account is likewise worth considering. The time an account has been open is an element in credit scores. A longer positive account is beneficial to credit scores. So, ending an older account in essence may have a more damaging impact.

Closing an account the correct way takes time, patience and organization. But it's crucial to be thorough in order to cancel your charge card properly.

To start the process of closing the account, accumulate and write down the customer service number and the mailing address you'll require. The 800 number is on your charge card, monthly statement and the issuer's site; the mailing address is likewise on the site and the monthly statement.

Closing a charge card that has a balance might not be the brightest thing to do. If you inform the card issuer that you're entertaining leaving, the lender may raise rates of interest on the owed balance. So pay off your charge card fully before you let the card issuer know you're leaving. Or, if you've been burned by a rate increase and you are able to find a balance transfer charge card with a better deal, shift the balance.

Once you get hold of the bank's customer service representative, begin by confirming that the balance on your charge card is "0". Don't assume that the balance is zero because you paid the full amount on your charge card bill. Interest stays on to accumulate between the time the issuer sent off the bill and when they got your check.

When you're sure the balance is "0", inform them that you're canceling the card. Although a few charge card companies will let you cancel without even talking to a representative, others might be less accommodating. Be prepared to have the customer service rep attempt and talk you out of closing your account. They'll be very convincing, so if this is what you chose, then tell them courteously once again by letting them know you wish the account closed at once.

For added confidence (just in case the customer service rep makes an error), write a short cancellation letter to the card issuer, addressed to the name provided. Request written verification of the account's closure. This is a must and is to be done in alignment with the telephone call. The letter ought to include your name, address, number and account number, and particulars from your earlier telephone call. Likewise, state that you wish your credit report to reflect that the account was "closed at the consumer's request."

Being additionally cautious isn't a bad thing. Enfolded with the letter, include the check number (or a copy of the canceled check or additional payment confirmation) that you used to pay for your account balance, as well as the date the check cleared your bank. Create a copy of the letter for your records. In addition, you are able to place your demolished charge card in the envelope with the letter. Send the letter thru certified mail or return receipt requested so you are able to prove the company got your letter.

Then you wait. Getting the card canceled might take a month or more, as a charge card issuer is a "big bureaucracy,".

After that time, have a look at a copy of your credit report to make certain the account is marked as "closed" on your credit report. If the account seems open, duplicate the process.

As you carry out the process of canceling your charge card, you might want to keep thorough notes on who you talked to, what they stated and when. That way, if anything fails, you'll have all the facts recorded. Once you get a return receipt from your certified mail, keep it with the log you're keeping and note the date the receipt comes in.

CHAPTER 9

INSTITUTE AUTOMATIC SAVINGS

Synopsis

Make a link from your checking account into a savings account that won't be touched. This may usually be done through the banks and automatic amounts will be transferred over every month. Most individuals won't put money into a savings account on a regular basis. They might wait till a large tax refund check arrives or another event to actually deposit money into savings, retirement, vacation, college, or additional accounts. If you institute an automatic savings deposit monthly, your accounts will start accumulating faster than you think.

Save Automatically

Do you have a savings account; all the same find it hard to find money to put into it? This isn't a rare problem and many individuals find it grueling to save. By and large when you receive income it's either straight off deposited into your checking account or you go to the bank to prepare a deposit. Generally these funds head straight to the checking account so they're available to pay for the seemingly perpetual flow of bills.

Many individuals save money as a second thought. When they get revenue the money is apportioned to bills, foodstuffs, rent or a mortgage or daily expenses among additional things. The only time supplying money to savings is when there is revenue left over. Regrettably with this backwards thinking there is just about never any revenue left over to save.

Once deposits are made into a savings account automatically and on a regular basis you don't have to think about it and the revenue is deposited prior to you having time to worry about expenses or how much money will be left over.

Thanks to innovative technology it is really simple to set up an automatic savings plan. If you presently have direct deposit through your employer or some other form of revenue you will find the most comfortable way to establish this is to have part of your money directly deposited into your savings account as well. It does not matter if it is ten dollars or five hundred dollars, merely having this happen automatically will guarantee money is saved every time you are paid.

If you do not have direct deposit there is still a simple option available if you do your banking at a local branch. Commonly your bank may link checking and saving accounts together and constitute automated transfers between accounts at a regular time interval that you select.

So if you cash your paycheck every other Friday, or receive other funds on a regular basis you may establish an automatic transfer of a set sum of money from checking to savings to co-occur with this deposit.

Wrapping Up

It all boils down to being organized and making smart decisions. Make certain your paid bills are organized in a container of some sort away from the rest of the house. Keep files for paid bills. Go through your files at the end of every year and throw away bills and receipts no longer needed for auditing purposes. Get hold of your local IRS office to see how long records need to be kept for audits. Generally federal tax return audits can be done 3 years back but cancelled checks might need to be kept for seven. Consult the Internet for auditing and records-keeping procedures for your state or region.

Follow the tips here and you will be well on your way to organizing your finances.

Printed by Libri Plureos GmbH in Hamburg, Germany